Livonia Public Library
CARL SANDBURG BRANCH #21
30100 W. 7 Mile Road
Livonia, Mich. 48152
248-893-4010

MEET THE GREATS

GERONIMO

TIM COOKE

Please visit our website, www.garethstevens.com.
For a free color catalog of all our high-quality books,
call toll free 1-800-542-2595 or fax 1-877-542-2596.

Cataloging-in-Publication Data

Names: Cooke, Tim.
Title: Geronimo / Tim Cooke.
Description: New York : Gareth Stevens Publishing, 2020. | Series: Meet the greats | Includes glossary and index.
Identifiers: ISBN 9781538252406 (pbk.) | ISBN 9781538252413 (library bound)
Subjects: LCSH: Geronimo, 1829-1909--Juvenile literature. | Apache Indians--Kings and rulers--Biography--Juvenile literature. | Apache Indians--Wars--Juvenile literature.
Classification: LCC E99.A6 C66 2020 | DDC 979'.004972 B--dc23

Published in 2020 by
Gareth Stevens Publishing
111 East 14th Street, Suite 349
New York, NY 10003

Copyright © 2020 Brown Bear Ltd

Picture credits: Front cover: Character artwork Supriya Sahai. Interior: Library of Congress: 13, 15b, 24, 25t, 28, 30, 33, 34, 35t, 38, 42b; Public Domain: Denver Library, 18, Denver Public Library/WH Martin, 39, Denver Library/A. Frank Randall, 10, Janet Lange & Hotelin-Hurel, 32, New York Public Library, 20, NYPL/ Digital Gallery Mid-Manhattan Picture Collection/Camillus Sidney, 21, Frank A. Rinehart, 42t, Mark A. Wilson/College of Wooster/Department of Geology, 12, 22; Shutterstock: Karel Bock, 25b, Ingrid Curry, 23, Everett Historical, 15t, 35, 40, 41, Looper5920, 43, LouLouPhotos, 29, Mark Stephens Photography, 8, Marzolino, 9, 14, Rafael Moreno, 11, Mountains Hunter, 31; US National Archives: Ben Witlick, 19.

Character artwork © Supriya Sahai
All other artworks © Brown Bear Books Ltd

All rights reserved. No part of this book may be reproduced in any form without permission from the publisher, except by a reviewer.

Printed in the United States of America

CPSIA compliance information: Batch #CW20GS: For further information contact Gareth Stevens,
New York, New York at 1-800-542-2595.

Contents

Introduction 4
Apache Upbringing 6
   Feature: Disappearing Territory 14
Warrior Leader 16
   Feature: Native American
   Reservations 24
The Last War 26
   Feature: Geronimo the Legend 34
Surrender and Celebrity 36
Timeline 44
Glossary 46
Further Resources 47
Index 48

Introduction

Born to a band of Apache in Mexico, Geronimo became one of the most feared Native American warriors.

The mention of Geronimo's name struck fear into white Americans all over the United States. At one time, Geronimo and a small group of warriors spent five years fighting U.S. forces. More than a quarter of the whole U.S. Army—5,000 soldiers—were sent to try to track him down, but Geronimo avoided capture. He launched raids on military **outposts** and white settlements before disappearing back into the deserts and mountains of the Southwest.

Geronimo was never an Apache **chief**, but he attracted people to follow him because of his skill as a warrior. He spent years defending the Apache's homelands. But even some Apache thought his violent campaign was not justified. By the time he finally surrendered, Geronimo was the last Apache, and one of the last Native Americans, fighting the U.S. government.

Apache
UPBRINGING

Geronimo was born at a time when settlers from Mexico and the United States were moving into the Apache's homelands.

Geronimo was born in June 1829 in No-Doyohn Canyon, which was then in Mexico but is now part of the U.S. state of Arizona. His original name was Goyaalé, or "the one who yawns." Geronimo was a nickname he gained later, after he became a warrior. Geronimo and his three brothers and four sisters belonged to the Bedonkohe, which was the smallest band of the Chiricahua tribe of Apache. Their grandfather had been a chief of the Bedonkohe. As was traditional, Geronimo was sent to live with another band of the Chiricahua, called the Tchihende.

MEET THE GREATS: **GERONIMO**

QUICK FACTS
- Geronimo came from a small band of the Chiricahua tribe of Apache.
- He became a warrior at the age of 17 and began taking part in raids on the Apache's neighbors.

The Apache lived in a dry landscape of mountains and rocky gorges.

APACHE BANDS

There were many bands of Chiricahua, who were just one of a number of different Apache tribes. The bands were based on extended families. They had their own leaders and usually lived separately. At times, they **cooperated** in order to trade or fight a common enemy. At other times, they fought each other. This situation could be confusing for people who dealt with the Apache, as different bands might be friendly or hostile toward them at the same time. There were many cases of **mistaken identity**, when one band was blamed for something another band had done.

A YOUNG HUNTER

The Apache lived in what are now Arizona and New Mexico. Their lives were based on hunting buffalo, which provided them with food and skins to make clothes and tents. The Apache also foraged, or collected wild berries and grasses for food. As Geronimo grew up, he became famed as a hunter. It was said that, when he killed his first animal, he ate its heart. The Apache believed this would bring him success on later hunts.

The Apache followed the buffalo herds that moved through the Southwest.

APACHE RAIDS

Life was hard for the Bedonkohe. For extra supplies, they raided their neighbors, who included not only Mexicans but also other native peoples, such as the Navajo and Comanche. Newcomers were gradually moving onto Apache land. Spaniards from Mexico and Americans from the East Coast arrived hoping to find gold or silver or to start cattle **ranches** in the green valleys.

Such people saw the Apache as fearsome thieves. Apache warriors attacked settlements or groups of travelers. They took what they needed and disappeared back into the landscape. They took their victims captive or killed them.

The Apache lived in dome-shaped shelters made from branches and grass.

The Apache often camped near sources of water, such as the Mimbres River of New Mexico.

Geronimo joined in Apache raids on other groups. He also married a young woman from the Nedni band named Alope. The couple had three children. In total, Geronimo would have nine wives.

CYCLE OF VIOLENCE

By the time Geronimo became a warrior, the Apache and the Mexicans were caught up in a cycle of raids. The Apache would carry out a raid on settlers, and the Mexican army would respond by attacking a band of Apache. Often, this was not even the same band that had carried out the raid. The second band of Apache would **retaliate** by carrying out their own raid on the Mexicans.

During the 1820s and 1830s, Apache raided around 100 settlements and killed some 5,000 Mexicans. The Mexican government offered a bounty, or reward, for anyone who killed an Apache. It would pay $25 for every Apache **scalp**. In response, Chiricahua led by the **war chief** Mangas Coloradas carried out more attacks on Mexican villages.

A FATEFUL JOURNEY

The Apache had good relations with some Mexicans. In 1851, Geronimo went south with a band led by Mangas Coloradas to trade with Mexicans in Chihuahua state. Geronimo took Alope, their three children, and his mother.

Apache Pass was a common route used by the Apache through the mountains of Arizona.

Temporary Apache camps had few defenses from attack.

The Apache carried buffalo **hides** and herbs to trade for knives, cloth, and beads. The Apache women stayed in their camp while the men went into the town of Janos to trade. While the men were away, Mexican soldiers attacked the camp and killed everyone who did not escape. The soldiers took the Apache's supplies and left.

When Geronimo returned from Janos, he found all of his family dead. He stood staring at the nearby river as the other Apache checked who else was dead. There were only 80 Apache, and Mangas Coloradas decided they could not fight a large group of Mexican soldiers. He forced Geronimo and the others to return home.

Disappearing TERRITORY

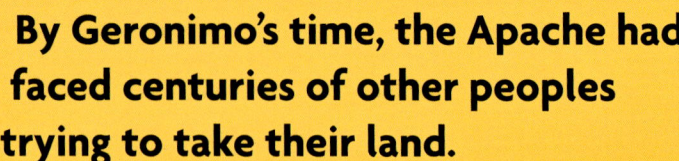

By Geronimo's time, the Apache had faced centuries of other peoples trying to take their land.

The first Spaniards began arriving on Apache land from Mexico as early as 1541. The newcomers broke up Apache trade with the **Pueblo** to the north. The Pueblo had traded crops and pottery with the Apache in exchange for buffalo meat and skins. Later, the Apache faced a new enemy. This was a native people called the Comanche, who were armed with European guns. The Comanche pushed the Apache from their traditional lands. The Apache moved south and west into the desert, where life was harder.

The Comanche hunted buffalo using bows and arrows or guns.

FEATURE: DISAPPEARING TERRITORY

After 1848, many settlers headed west in large groups called wagon trains.

In the 1840s, Apache territory came under threat again. After the Mexican–American War (1846–1848), their land passed from Mexican control to the United States. This encouraged the arrival of white settlers from the east. The discovery of gold in California in 1848 also led settlers to head west. They hoped to find new sources of valuable **minerals**. As settlers arrived, so did telegraph lines, railroads, and soldiers. For the Apache, the arrival of settlers would lead to decades of fighting to try to defend their land.

Settlers set up farms to grow crops in the open plains.

Warrior LEADER

After the tragedy of losing his family, Geronimo spent the next three decades in an almost constant state of war.

When he got home, Geronimo burned all his family's possessions. As he sat crying in the desert, he thought he heard the voice of the Apache god Usen. Usen said, "No gun will ever kill you. I will take the bullets from the guns of the Mexicans so they will have nothing but powder, and I will guide your arrows." Geronimo took the message as a sign that he should become a warrior. He later said, "I was never again contented in our happy home, and whenever I saw anything to remind me of former happy days my heart would ache for revenge on Mexico."

MEET THE GREATS: **GERONIMO**

QUICK FACTS
- The murder of his family made Geronimo determined to fight the Mexicans.
- His first contact with white Americans was friendly, but the friendly relations did not last.

After Alope's death, Geronimo married another eight times. Ta-ayz-slath was his fifth or sixth wife.

OUT FOR REVENGE

Geronimo's anger changed his life. When Mangas Coloradas called together his warriors to discuss how to react to the **massacre** at Janos, everyone listened respectfully to Geronimo's ideas. Mangas Coloradas sent him to ask other Apache bands to help them. Geronimo visited Cochise, chief of the Chiricahua. The Chiricahua decided to join Mangas Coloradas, because they did not want the Mexicans to attack more Apache bands. Geronimo also got the support of Alope's band, the Nedni.

A NEW NAME

In January 1852, the Apache warriors gathered to attack Mexican soldiers in a town called Arizpe, in Sonora. Because Geronimo had lost his family, he led the raid. Geronimo hid the Apache warriors in rocks near the town and sent others to **lure** the Mexican soldiers out of town.

Geronimo attacked the Mexicans for two hours. He fought so hard that the Mexican soldiers who saw him called out, "Look out! Geronimo!" It might have been that they were calling in Spanish on Saint Jerome to protect them. Whatever they meant, the name stuck. Soon the Apache also called Goyaalé "Geronimo."

This photograph taken later in Geronimo's life shows him dressed as a warrior with his rifle. He was an expert shot.

U.S. Cavalry attack an Apache village in this imaginary scene.

RAIDING IN MEXICO

Geronimo went on to lead more raids against Mexican villages. He also led the defense of his own village when it was attacked by Mexican soldiers. Soon afterward, he commanded 25 warriors in an **ambush** of Mexican soldiers in a mountain pass. The Apache killed every soldier, but they lost many men themselves. Geronimo became more careful in choosing his targets. He continued to lead war raids into Mexico, killing Mexicans and returning home with stolen supplies. His reputation as a warrior was growing.

A NEW ENEMY

Soon, however, Geronimo faced a new enemy. In 1858, he met his first white Americans when he came across some men mapping the land. The Apache and the **surveyors** could not speak each other's languages, but they traded some goods and even camped near one another. More white Americans followed the surveyors, however. These newcomers did not trust the Apache, and the Apache did not trust them. The Apache feared these new arrivals were trying to take their land.

Most of Geronimo's warriors did not have horses. They walked or ran long distances over the plains.

Cochise and his warriors defeated a small U.S. force in the Dragoon Mountains of Arizona—but were later defeated.

CONFLICT WITH THE U.S. ARMY

In 1861, some Apache raided a ranch. They stole 20 cows and took away a 12-year-old boy named Felix Ward. The U.S. Army set out to track them and followed them to Apache Pass. The soldiers wrongly thought that the Apache were Chiricahua and questioned the Chiricahua chief, Cochise, who was Geronimo's father-in-law. Cochise denied having anything to do with the raid. The two sides argued, and the U.S. Army hanged some Apache for killing Americans. In return, the Apache attacked and killed workers building a mail route for settlers.

COCHISE LEADS THE WAY

A long period of tension began between the U.S. Army and the Apache led by Cochise and his ally, Mangas Coloradas. The Apache attacked small groups of American soldiers and settlers. However, Cochise was eager for peace. He could see that it was impossible to turn back the tide of white settlers. After the Apache had hidden in the mountains for years, Cochise agreed to make peace with the Americans. He said that the Chiricahua would move onto a **reservation** in some of the best land in Apache territory, near Apache Pass.

Cochise was prepared to give up some Apache land in return for being left to live in peace on a reservation.

Native American RESERVATIONS

The reservation at Apache Pass was just one of the special areas created for Native Americans by the U.S. government.

The government was eager to open the West for settlement. Settlers wanted to build towns and to fence off the plains to create farms. That brought them into conflict with Native Americans and their traditional ways of life. The government decided to move Native Americans onto areas of land called reservations. This land would be protected from settlement.

Life on the reservation was hard, and food was in short supply.

FEATURE: NATIVE AMERICAN RESERVATIONS

Native peoples on reservations dealt with Indian agents (left) who acted on behalf of the U.S. government.

However, the land selected for reservations was often of poor quality. As happened with the Apache, the government sometimes also forced native groups who were very different from one another to live together.

Living on a reservation was particularly hard for groups such as the Apache, who depended on the buffalo for their food, clothing, and other goods. These peoples followed the buffalo herds as they moved around. On the reservation, it was impossible to follow the buffalo. Anyone who left the reservation to do so was branded an outlaw. They could be hunted and captured by the U.S. Army.

Buffalo **migrated** over the plains as they searched for food and water.

25

The Last WAR

Geronimo moved onto the reservation at Apache Pass, but when the government changed the deal, he changed his mind.

Geronimo was disappointed when Cochise agreed to lead the Chiricahua to the reservation, but he went along with his people. Only a few years later, however, in 1874, Cochise died. Now the U.S. government canceled the agreement it had made with him. It wanted the land at Apache Pass for white settlers and to open mines. It said that the Apache had to move north to the San Carlos Reservation. The land there was poor, and life would be very hard. Some Apache did not want to fight anymore and agreed to move. However, about two-thirds of the Apache refused to go.

Geronimo (right) led a number of Apache who did not want to live on the reservation.

A BROKEN DEAL

Geronimo was angry that the government had changed its deal. He fled with about 400 other Chiricahua to the Sierra Madre mountains in northern Mexico. They went back to their raiding lifestyle. This meant they were now targets for the U.S. Army as well as the Mexicans. In 1873, Mexican troops attacked Geronimo's settlement. In return, the Apache moved farther into Mexico, where they spent a year raiding villages in Sonora state. In one battle, Apache warriors and Mexican soldiers faced each other at a place called White Hill. The Apache charged the surprised soldiers, and killed everyone who was too slow to get away.

ON THE RESERVATION

Geronimo lived in the mountains for a decade, moving between Mexico and Arizona. In 1877, however, he was captured and placed in chains. He and his followers were taken to the San Carlos Reservation in southeastern Arizona.

Conditions were terrible. The soil was too poor for **agriculture**, so the Apache had to depend on the government for food. In addition, different bands of Apache lived on the reservation, with their own leaders and traditions. Some of these bands had never gotten along and did not do so now.

The land of the San Carlos Reservation was dry and rocky.

Geronimo hated the reservation. He would spend nearly a decade escaping, but that brought him and his followers into conflict with both the U.S. Army and Mexican troops.

TRICKED!

In 1880, Geronimo and his warriors killed 24 Mexican soldiers who attacked their camp in the mountains. Soon Geronimo and a handful of warriors were facing three companies of soldiers. The Apache had no choice but to run. They later agreed to make peace, but the Mexicans tricked them. They gave the Apache liquor and made them drunk before they killed 20 Apache and the others ran away.

This illustration shows Apache warriors returning from a raid in Mexico with stolen horses.

It was illegal to sell guns or ammunition to Native Americans, but the law was widely broken.

EXPERT SHOT

The Apache returned to the reservation, but soon they were back in Mexico raiding and fighting. Geronimo and his followers used guns they had obtained by illegal trade, because no one was supposed to sell weapons to Native Americans. Geronimo was an expert shot with a rifle, and usually carried either a Springfield 1873 or a Winchester 1876. During his military campaign, Geronimo was wounded a total of eight times. He was shot in the arm, leg, face, back, and side, and was slashed with swords.

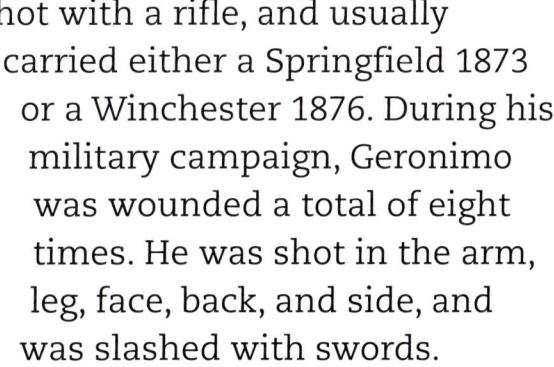

UNDER PRESSURE

In 1884, Geronimo headed back from Mexico to Arizona to try to **recruit** more followers. He was not successful. What was more, he was attacked by U.S. soldiers and some of his warriors were killed. Geronimo found himself in danger of being trapped between the Americans to the north and the Mexicans to the south. He decided it would be better to fight the Mexicans on their own, so he headed south. When the Mexican army found his band, a gun battle broke out that lasted all day.

In the second half of the 1800s, the Mexican army fought American and French forces, as well as the Apache.

Geronimo (left, on horse) escaped death a number of times—but he was running out of energy to keep fighting.

 At one time during the battle, Geronimo was hiding in a ditch near the Mexican commander. He said in his autobiography that he heard the Mexican general tell his men, "Over there is the red devil Geronimo and his hated band. This must be his last day … Take no prisoners; dead Indians is what we want." Geronimo said that in reply he shot and killed the general. The Apache fought until darkness fell, then slipped away from the battlefield. Time was running out for Geronimo and his followers.

Geronimo
THE LEGEND

Geronimo was not the only Native American who resisted white settlement, but he became one of the best known—and the most feared.

Geronimo's reputation spread in the late 1880s. Newspaper reports carried dramatic descriptions of the warrior and his band, calling them "savage beasts" and saying that they left "a trail of blood." The public seemed to enjoy the horror of reading about Geronimo's campaign against white settlers. The government was happy for Geronimo to have such a bad reputation, because it made it easier to claim the Apache had to be controlled to keep American settlers on the **frontier** safe. Generals told their soldiers the only way to tame the West was by capturing or killing the Apache leader.

This poster advertises a Wild West show put on by Pawnee Bill, a showman who later hired Geronimo for his shows.

FEATURE: GERONIMO THE LEGEND

Geronimo (center) appeared with other Apache at the St. Louis World's Fair in 1904.

Geronimo's legend spread so widely that, after his capture, he became a popular tourist attraction in the East. He featured in stories and paintings. His name became a shorthand for **atrocities** committed against white settlers.

In captivity in 1906, Geronimo was persuaded to **dictate** his own story to a local teacher. Geronimo's **autobiography** became a best seller. He explained his point of view that he was defending the Apache. He claimed that he acted from a sense of honor. In Geronimo's version of events, it was not he who could not be trusted, but the U.S. Army and their government.

Geronimo earned money by selling photographs of himself like this one to curious tourists.

Surrender and
CELEBRITY

Geronimo's campaigns made him famous. When he finally surrendered, he became a national celebrity.

Geronimo believed he was fighting to preserve the Apache way of life. To many Americans, however, he was a criminal who used violence to resist inevitable change in the American West. To the American government, he was an enemy who had to be stopped. Geronimo's clashes with the U.S. Army were widely reported in newspapers across the United States. He was so skilled at hiding with his followers that more than 5,000 soldiers had no luck in finding him. This made Americans very frightened. It seemed that there was no force that could stop him.

MEET THE GREATS: GERONIMO

QUICK FACTS

❀ After Geronimo's surrender, he spent the rest of his life as a prisoner.

❀ He was a popular attraction in shows and exhibitions.

Geronimo meets U.S. soldiers to discuss his surrender.

FINAL SURRENDER

In the end, Geronimo realized that he could not continue fighting. On September 4, 1886, he surrendered for the last time. In the account of his life Geronimo wrote later, he said that he regretted his decision. He wrote, "I should never have surrendered. I should have fought until I was the last man alive."

Geronimo surrendered to General Nelson Miles in Skeleton Canyon in Arizona. Miles arranged a treaty outlining the terms of Geronimo's surrender.

The warrior chief and about 400 of his followers were put on a train under guard by U.S. soldiers. They were transported across the country to Florida, where they were imprisoned in Fort Pickens in Pensacola Bay.

There had been no Native American attacks in Florida for more than 30 years, so people in the state were fascinated by the idea of the "savage" warriors from the West. Tourists came to try to see Geronimo and his companions, as if they were exhibits. The Apache proved a popular attraction with visitors. When the Apache were moved to Alabama two years later, the local Florida newspaper complained that a "large-sized curiosity" was being taken away.

In captivity, Geronimo mainly lived quietly with his former followers.

ON DISPLAY

In Alabama, many of the Apache died from tuberculosis, a disease made worse by the damp climate of the Deep South. In 1894, Geronimo was moved to Fort Sill in Oklahoma, which would be his home for the rest of his life.

Although Geronimo was kept under armed guard, he was not locked in a cell. In 1898, he appeared at the Omaha Exhibition. He was among some Apache who demonstrated traditional dancing for visitors. Some of the visitors were disappointed, however. They were not really interested in the Apache. They had hoped to see a man who looked and acted more like a notorious killer.

This photograph claims to show Geronimo skinning his last buffalo—in fact, the event was staged on a ranch in 1905.

President William McKinley addresses a crowd at the Pan-American Exposition in Buffalo, where Geronimo appeared in 1901.

RAISING MONEY

Geronimo appeared in public again at the 1901 Pan-American Exposition in Buffalo, New York. This time he took part in faked fights in which Native Americans fought against U.S. cavalry.

Geronimo enjoyed being famous, and in 1904 he agreed to appear at the World's Fair in St. Louis, Missouri. This time he was part of the **ethnology** exhibit, which highlighted differences between peoples of the world. Geronimo made extra money by signing his autograph and selling photographs. People were prepared to pay for a souvenir of the feared war chief. Later, Geronimo also sold buttons from his coat. He became quite wealthy, and used some of his money to pay for education for Apache children.

Geronimo joined a Wild West Show, where he appeared in scenes that portrayed Native Americans as **ruthless** killers. Rather than learning about Apache traditions, many white Americans preferred the thrill of seeing the warriors act as they imagined they had acted on the frontier.

Many Americans were disappointed to find that Geronimo was a quiet old man.

VISIT TO WASHINGTON

When Theodore Roosevelt became U.S. president in 1905, he invited Geronimo to represent the Apache at his **inauguration**. Geronimo and five other Native American chiefs rode their horses in the parade along Pennsylvania Avenue. Geronimo had another reason to want to go to Washington, DC, however. While he was there, he had a private meeting with Roosevelt.

Geronimo and other Native American chiefs ride down Pennsylvania Avenue in 1905.

Geronimo was buried at Fort Sill, where his grave remains a monument for many Native Americans.

Geronimo tried to get Roosevelt to let the Apache return to their homeland in Arizona. Roosevelt refused. He said the Apache had behaved too badly toward white settlers in Arizona.

In February 1909, Geronimo was thrown off his horse in Oklahoma. He spent a cold night lying on the ground. Geronimo got sick and died six days later, on February 17. He was 79 years old.

Geronimo was buried at Fort Sill, but his name was still heard often. Parents would frighten naughty children by threatening that Geronimo would get them. In World War II, more than 30 years after Geronimo's death, U.S. airborne soldiers went into battle shouting as their war cry the name of the army's former enemy: "Geronimo!"

Timeline

1829	• Born in June in present-day Arizona, he is given the name Goyaalé.
1835	• The Mexican authorities offer a reward for every Apache scalp.
1846	• Geronimo becomes a warrior after he turns 17. He marries his first wife, Alope.
1848	• Apache territory passes from Mexican control to the United States at the end of the Mexican–American War.
1858	• Alope, their three children, and Geronimo's mother are killed by Mexican troops near the town of Janos. When leading a revenge attack, Geronimo first earns his nickname.
1873	• Geronimo makes peace with the Mexicans at Casas Grandes, but they trick him and murder some of his followers.
1874	• Cochise dies, and the government moves the Apache to a reservation at San Carlos.
1876	• Geronimo and his followers head to Mexico to escape from the San Carlos Reservation.
1877	• Geronimo is captured and returned to San Carlos.
1878	• Geronimo again leads an escape from the reservation to the mountains of Mexico.
1881	• Geronimo leaves the reservation again.
1885	• Geronimo leaves the reservation for Mexico for the final time.

1886 • Geronimo finally surrenders to General Nelson A. Miles at Skeleton Canyon. He and his followers are eventually sent by train to Florida, where they become a tourist attraction.

1887 • The Apache are sent to Mount Vernon Barracks in Alabama, where many die from tuberculosis.

1894 • Geronimo and his followers arrive in Fort Sill in Oklahoma.

1898 • Geronimo appears at an exhibition in Omaha, Nebraska. He will appear in a number of similar exhibitions over the next decade.

1904 • Geronimo appears at the World's Fair in St. Louis. He agrees to appear in Pawnee Bill's Wild West Show.

1905 • Geronimo joins the inaugural parade for President Theodore Roosevelt's second term, but fails to get Roosevelt to allow the Apache to return home.

1906 • Geronimo's autobiography is published.

1909 • Dies at Fort Sill on February 17.

NOTABLE APPEARANCES
- Trans-Mississippi International Exposition (1898)
- St. Louis World's Fair (1904)
- President Roosevelt's Inaugural Parade (1905)

Glossary

agriculture Growing crops and raising animals.

ambush A surprise attack by hidden attackers.

atrocities Very wicked and cruel acts.

autobiography A written account of someone's own life.

chief The usual leader of a Native American band.

cooperated Worked together for a particular purpose.

dictate To speak something aloud so it can be written down.

ethnology The study of peoples and their differences and similarities.

frontier The boundary of the United States as the country spread westward.

hides The skins of animals such as buffalo.

inauguration A ceremony held when a new president takes office.

lure To trick someone into going somewhere.

massacre The violent killing of many people.

migrated Moved from place to place with the seasons.

minerals Solid natural substances used to make things.

mistaken identity When someone is wrongly identified.

outposts Isolated military forts.

Pueblo Native people who lived in parts of modern-day Arizona, New Mexico, and Texas.

ranches Large farms for raising cattle.

recruit To gather new members of a group.

reservation An area set aside for Native Americans.

retaliate To make an attack in return for a similar attack.

ruthless Acting without pity.

scalp The skin on the head.

surveyors People who mapped the land.

war chief A Native American military leader.

Further Resources

Books

Dell, Pamela. *Apache Resistance: Causes and Effects of Geronimo's Campaign.* Cause and Effect: American Indian History. North Mankato, MN: Capstone Press, 2015.

Freedman, Jeri. *Geronimo: Leader of Native American Resistance.* Hero or Villain?: Claims and Counterclaims. New York: Cavendish Square Publishing, 2018.

Haugen, Brenda. *Geronimo: The Inspiring Life Story of an Apache Warrior.* Inspiring Stories. Minneapolis, MN: Compass Point Books, 2016.

Lowery, Linda. *Native Peoples of the Southwest.* North American Indian Nations. Minneapolis, MN: Lerner Publications, 2016.

Websites

Apache
www.britannica.com/topic/Apache-people
An account of the lives and history of the Apache and their descendants.

Biography
www.biography.com/political-figure/geronimo
A biography of Geronimo.

Reservation
www.history.com/this-day-in-history/geronimo-flees-arizona-reservation
An article about Geronimo's life on the San Carlos Reservation.

Timeline
geronimoapachewarrior.weebly.com/timeline.html
A timeline of important dates in Geronimo's life.

Publisher's note to educators and parents: Our editors have carefully reviewed these websites to ensure that they are suitable for students. Many websites change frequently, however, and we cannot guarantee that a site's future contents will continue to meet our high standards of quality and educational value. Be advised that students should be closely supervised whenever they access the Internet.

Index

A
agriculture 29
Alabama 39, 40
Alope 11, 12, 18
Apache 4, 8, 9, 11, 12, 18, 19, 20, 21, 25, 26, 29, 36, 43
Apache Pass 12, 22, 23, 24, 26
Arizona 6, 9, 22, 29, 32, 43
Arizpe 19
autobiography, Geronimo 35

B
Bedonkohe 6, 10
buffalo 9, 13, 14, 25, 40

C
Chihuahua state 12
Chiricahua 6, 8, 12, 18, 22, 23, 26, 28
Cochise 18, 22, 23, 26
Comanche 10, 14

D F
Dragoon Mountains 22
Florida 39
Fort Pickens 39
Fort Sill 40, 43
frontier 34

G
Geronimo, name 19
gold 10, 15
Goyaalé, name 6
guns 16, 31

H
horses 21, 30
hunting 9

I J
Indian agents 25
Janos massacre 13, 18

M
Mangas Coloradas 12, 13, 18, 23
Mexican American War 15
Mexican Army 11, 30, 32
Mexico 6, 28, 29, 31
Miles, Nelson 38

N
Native Americans 10, 14
Navajo 10
New Mexico 9
newspapers and Geronimo 36, 34

O P
Oklahoma 40, 43
Omaha Exhibition 40
Pan-American Exposition 41
public appearances 35, 39, 40, 41, 42
Pueblo 14

R
raids 4, 10, 11, 20, 28, 30, 31
ranches 10
reputation, Geronimo's 34, 35
reservations 23, 24–25, 26, 29, 30, 31
Roosevelt, Theodore 42, 43

S
San Carlos Reservation 26, 29
settlers 6, 10, 15, 24, 26
Sierra Madre 28
Sonora 19, 28
souvenirs, of Geronimo 41
Spaniards 10, 14
St. Louis World's Fair 35, 41
surrender, Geronimo 4, 38
surveyors, white 21

T
Ta-ayz-slath 18
tourist attraction, Geronimo as 35, 39
trade, Apache 14

U
U.S. Army 4, 22, 23, 25, 28, 30, 36
U.S. Cavalry 20, 41
Usen 16

W
Ward, Felix 22
warriors, Apache 19
Washington, DC 42
West 36, 39
White Hill 28
Wild West show 35, 42
World's Fair, St. Louis 35, 41